...from dog lovers,
Peter + Marilena

D0011835

by R. D. Rosen
Harry Prichett
Rob Battles

bad dog

Workman
Publishing,
New York

Library of Congress Cataloging-in-
Publication Data is available.

ISBN-13: 978-0-7611-3983-6
ISBN-10: 0-7611-3983-4

Photo editor: John Blum

Workman books are available at special
discounts when purchased in bulk for
premiums and sales promotions as well
as for fund-raising or educational use.
Special editions of book excerpts can
also be created to specification. For
details, contact the Special Sales
Director at the address below.

Workman Publishing Company, Inc.
708 Broadway
New York, NY 10003-9555
www.workman.com

Printed in China
First printing September 2005

10 9 8 7 6 5 4 3

to Sparky, Suka,
Duane, Bubba, Tina,
Honey Bear, Maurice,
Clarke, Fang, Ella,
Louis, Tiny, and Slimy

May they all rest
in peace.

Introduction

Sooner or later, every dog owner utters the words "Bad dog!"

If you only knew how bad. Wake up, dog "owners"—it's time to embrace the whole dog, not just the phony side that pretends to like you by wagging its tail in the foyer every time you come home. Best friend? Please.

Because inside every slobbering basset hound, wheezing pug, or trembling Chihuahua is a bad dog. Sometimes a very bad dog. Just waiting to get out.

Did we say "waiting"? Oops. The following pages suggest otherwise. So sit. Stay. And learn some new tricks. Because these dogs don't roll over for anybody.

R. D. Rosen
Harry Prichett
Rob Battles

"Does this dress make me look fat?"

NAME: Peanut

AGE: 1

HOBBY: Admiring rock gardens

"Third room to the left,
honey. The Chihuahua in
the teddy."

NAME: Beverly

AGE: 5

HOBBY: Making jewelry out of
sea glass

"I just had a look at your MRI, Mrs. Horowitz, and I'm afraid the news isn't good."

NAME: Max

AGE: 9

HOBBY: Twitching while asleep

"Just once, I wish *he'd* sniff *my* butt."

NAME: Chester

AGE: 10

HOBBY: Playing Celtic fiddle

"Come here, little girl, and let Santa slobber on you."

NAME: Butchie

AGE: 9

HOBBY: Collecting cigar stubs

"If I look a little nervous
up here tonight, you're not
imagining things. I've
just had a small bowel
movement in my pants."

NAME: Pongo

AGE: 7

HOBBY: Listening to
relaxation tapes

"You'll probably want to
bury my treasure."

NAME: Taffy
AGE: 4
HOBBY: Tweaking my piña
colada recipes

"Thanks for having me in.
Are you familiar with the
new *Britannica*?"

NAME: Stewart

AGE: 4

HOBBY: Thumb wrestling

"Huh? What? Who's in heat?"

NAME: Spanky

AGE: 3

HOBBY: Creating gourmet fertilizer

"Since Frank's been gone,
it's just me and the
painkillers."

NAME: Honey

AGE: 9

HOBBY: Antiquarian books

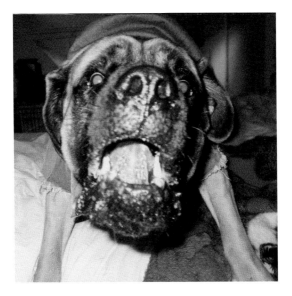

"C'mon, sweet cakes, how about a little kiss for the skipper?"

NAME: Sampson
AGE: 14
HOBBY: Trawling

"Somebody's got to wear the pants in this friggin' family."

NAME: Duke

AGE: 1

HOBBY: Shopping for vintage shoes

"The difference between
lovable old me and a
hideous creature is just
half an inch of gum."

NAME: Ricky
AGE: 8 months
HOBBY: Groveling

"I used to be a croupier.
Now I'm just a crapier."

NAME: Andy Moog

AGE: 4

HOBBY: Looking at old travel
brochures

"Sure, it slows me down, but it sets me apart from the other dogs at the track."

NAME: Curly

AGE: 9

HOBBY: Making dream catchers

"These colors don't run,
but I do."

NAME: Scraps

AGE: 1

HOBBY: Arguing without facts

"So you're Crystal. Word is you really know how to please a corgi."

NAME: Kaiju

AGE: 2

HOBBY: Listening to Hank Williams Sr.

"At this school, Mr. Wilcox, one does not drag one's hindquarters across the carpet."

NAME: Bailey

AGE: 14

HOBBY: Howling show tunes

"I smell a rodeo."

NAME: Angela

AGE: 6

HOBBY: Chasing conestogas

"When you sniff as many
dogs as I do, you need
some protection."

NAME: Larry

AGE: 7

HOBBY: Mixology

"Pour yourself another hot toddy while I slip out of my parka."

NAME: Little Nell

AGE: 6

HOBBY: Barking at chairlift operators

"These are just a few of my wives."

NAMES: (l. to r.) Frita, Brita, Riley, Jade, and Goody
AGES: 9, 7, 4, 2, 2 months
HOBBY: The Tabernacle Dog Choir

"I'm not laughing on the inside, either."

NAME: Philly
AGE: 2
HOBBY: Squirrel taxidermy

"Not tonight. I have worms."

NAMES: Onyx and Willy

AGES: 7, 6

HOBBY: Hosting sit-down dinner parties

"It hurts me that the
other dogs won't let me
play with them."

NAME: Max

AGE: 13

HOBBY: Amateur meteorologist

"Wait a second. I don't understand my costume."

NAME: Sprinkles

AGE: 1

HOBBY: Bottling my own water

"I don't say this lightly:
I believe I was born to
play Pocahontas."

NAME: Annie

AGE: 9

HOBBY: Gravestone rubbing

"How about one more for the road, Rocco?"

NAME: Alfredo

AGE: 5

HOBBY: Vomiting on the mail

"I just serve drinks.
That's as far as I'll go."

NAME: Petunia

AGE: 5

HOBBY: Giving French manicures

"I'm afraid I have some bad news. I'm not really a doctor."

NAME: Beau

AGE: 9

HOBBY: Collecting vintage scalpels

"The elders have spoken.
Welcome to the Order of
the Vested Shih Tzus."

NAME: Barley

AGE: 4

HOBBY: Barking in tongues

"My brother just got out of
Betty Ford."

NAMES: Travis and Tex

AGES: 4

HOBBIES: Making growl
recordings; playing
checkers

"Shabbat Shalom. Please take a seat. The service is about to begin."

NAME: Aaron

AGE: 3

HOBBY: Disguising pork as chicken

"As soon as I make enough
money, I'm going to send
for my sister."

NAME: Masha

AGE: 4

HOBBY: Scrimping

"Snap it already! It's hard to hold these smiles."

NAMES: Adam and Dexter

AGES: 4

HOBBY: Speed dating

"You can put dollar bills in my collar, ladies, but don't touch the merchandise."

NAME: Kodi

AGE: 4

HOBBY: Hot room yoga

"And this one, class, is called Downward Facing Moron."

NAME: Dallas

AGE: 2

HOBBY: Disney character topiary

"I knew he wouldn't show."

NAME: Elsie

AGE: 5

HOBBY: Collecting snow globes

"Get your own damn breakfast!"

NAME: Esther

AGE: 5

HOBBY: Chewing pencils

"Here's the deal--I soil the afghan, you pay me, I leave."

NAME: Bosco

AGE: 1

HOBBY: Humping performance fleece

"Here's what I want for my birthday: Don't treat me like this the rest of the year."

NAME: Scout

AGE: 1

HOBBY: Licking cake while it's cooling

"When I first started in showbiz, I had dreams. Now all I've got is a mortgage and dental bills."

NAME: Lana

AGE: 8 months

HOBBY: Knocking over plants

"Do you like it? I did it myself."

NAME: Zoe

AGE: 2

HOBBY: Fighting regret

"After a long day sniffing baggage, all I ask for is a little respect at home. Now bring me another cold one."

NAME: Ron

AGE: 6

HOBBY: Walking on hind legs as if it's nothing

"What I like about trees is that there's no commitment."

NAME: Ernie

AGE: 3

HOBBY: Watching *Pimp My Ride*

"These piñata parties make me nervous."

NAME: Cindy Lou

AGE: 4

HOBBY: Sleeping on lingerie

"Listen to me! I am *not* a bird. I am *not* a plane. I'm just your dog, Charlie."

NAME: Charlie

AGE: 1

HOBBY: Whittling totems

"Don't screw with me, Arnie--I was making deals 30 years before you even *heard* of film school."

NAME: Gizzy

AGE: 5

HOBBY: Licking head shots

"My dream? To open for
Celine Dion. My reality:
Jared Cooper's seventh
birthday party."

NAME: Natty-Boh

AGE: 2

HOBBY: Swallowing loose change

49

"I may be rich, but I still like to sniff a fire hydrant now and then."

NAME: Gumbo

AGE: 4

HOBBY: Biting knee-jerk liberals

"After a thorough investigation, Mr. Timmons, I've discovered black mold in the basement."

NAME: Casanova
AGE: 2
HOBBY: Bookbinding

"The only thing I don't like about good weed is the dry mouth."

NAMES: **Harley and Teddy**
AGES: **10, 6**
HOBBY: **Baking from scratch**

"I wonder if the real
President Lincoln had worms."

"I'd give you a lap dance
if I knew how to get on
your lap."

NAME: Jasmine

AGE: 3

HOBBY: Getting seaweed wraps

"For my next illusion, I'm going to make our sadistic owners, Scott and Julie, disappear."

NAMES: Macy and Baxter
AGES: 7, 8
HOBBY: Naked Twister

"I'm not even sure it's my own tongue."

NAME: Abby

AGE: 1

HOBBY: Collecting rabbit remains

"Forbidden love is twice as sweet."

NAME: Lacy J
AGE: 9 months
HOBBY: Violently chewing hind leg

"Honey, I've been doing this with you for twelve years, and I still have no idea what 'Renaissance Festival' means."

NAMES: Bailey and Daphne
AGES: 5, 4
HOBBY: Contract bridge

"Sister Pauline, whenever
I'm with you I want to
smell your secret place.
Is that wrong?"

NAMES: Pauline and Vincent
AGES: 16, 3
HOBBY: Online Scrabble

"I use the income from my
catalog modeling to
support my habit."

NAME: Jack

AGE: 4

HOBBY: Pickling

"I doo-doo."

NAME: Scarlett
AGE: 2
HOBBY: Police auctions

"How about a taste of this, sailor?"

NAME: Miz Skeeter Bug
AGE: 2
HOBBY: Scrimshaw

"You may want to consider washing this load again."

NAME: Olive
AGE: 7 months
HOBBY: Cha-cha competitions

"Take that damn toilet
paper out of my trees!"

NAME: Indiana

AGE: 3

HOBBY: Creating unusual
pizza topping combinations

"Sweet mother of mercy--the Viagra's working!"

NAME: Sam

AGE: 8

HOBBY: Barking in Portuguese

"Young dogs nowadays don't understand old money."

NAME: Keena
AGE: 14
HOBBY: Reading Eudora Welty

"I married a Jew."

NAME: Hollis

AGE: 7

HOBBY: Tie-dyeing yarmulkes

"Halloween, my ass."

NAME: Monet
AGE: 10 months
HOBBY: Hating Frisbees

"Frank, I want you and
Louie to work it out. There's
no room in the family for
disputes over who gets to
lick whose genitals."

NAME: Carmella

AGE: 5 months

HOBBY: Spreading ugly gossip
at the dog run

"It's odd to think that there isn't an inch of this yard that I haven't relieved myself on."

NAME: Sherlock

AGE: 9

HOBBY: Sponge painting

"Sure, they *say* he's stuffed,
but you'd never know it by
the way we make love."

NAME: Punch

AGE: 6

HOBBY: Designing rubber toys

"I'm getting too old for this shit."

NAME: Anabelle

AGE: 9

HOBBY: Scat singing

"How many times do I have to tell you?! My name is Pete. Not Mr. Dibbles."

NAME: Mr. Dibbles

AGE: 1

HOBBY: Laminating old menus

"I thought I told you not to wake me when I'm napping."

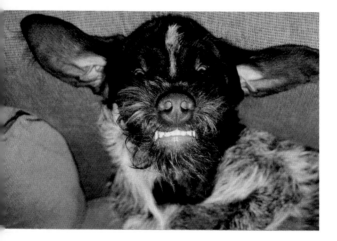

NAME: Duncan

AGE: 3

HOBBY: Extreme camping

"I want a divorce, Oscar.
You can have the plastic
car."

NAMES: Oscar and Norma

AGES: 3

HOBBIES: Whimpering and
bickering

"My bark is even worse
than my bike."

NAME: Buddy

AGE: 4

HOBBY: Pretending to smoke
Lucky Strikes

"Last year we went as
weapons of mass urination."

NAMES: Abigail, Maynard,
Chet, and Ginger
AGES: 1, 2, 2, 1
HOBBY: Busting screen doors

"Would you like to touch
my giblets?"

NAME: Seymour

AGE: 4

HOBBY: Feigning deafness

"If our owner only had a brain."

NAMES: Dandee, Tabby, Maddie, and Remy
AGES: 9, 4, 2, 2
HOBBY: Silently plotting revenge

"I have no idea what Pee
Wee's issues are. I'm just
glad he wears a diaper."

NAME: Lady

AGE: 8

HOBBY: Calling vets and
hanging up

"Protecting the universe is
a lonely business."

NAME: Lexie

AGE: 2

HOBBY: Scanning horizons

"Satan is my master now."

NAME: Penny

AGE: 8

HOBBY: Mesmerizing visitors

"Hey! You with the flea
collar! Go take a dump in
your own yard!"

NAME: Bianca

AGE: 6

HOBBY: Knitting on the front
stoop

"Does this sweater make me look gay?"

NAME: Duke

AGE: 11

HOBBY: Admiring my jawline

"Does this sweater make me look straight?"

NAME: Scamp

AGE: 7 months

HOBBY: Composting

"This must be what they mean by 'kickin' in.'"

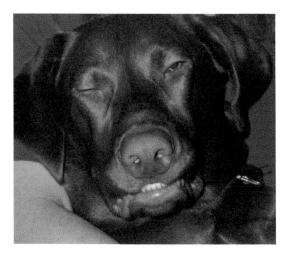

NAME: Ernie
AGE: 8 months
HOBBY: Chasing parked cars

"Take me."

NAME: Lila
AGE: 8 weeks
HOBBY: Hair braiding

"Dramamine makes me sad."

NAME: Bow

AGE: 4

HOBBY: Soprano saxophone

"Don't get excited, honey,
it's part of the costume."

NAME: Donald

AGE: 8

HOBBY: Listening to police-
band radio

"I hate living here. These people bore me."

NAME: Wendell

AGE: 1

HOBBY: Belching the alphabet

"These backup singers suck."

NAME: Ruppert

AGE: 6

HOBBY: Merengue dancing

"The sex therapist says we should try a cushion."

NAMES: Buck and Zesty
AGES: 7, 1
HOBBY: Night clamming

"I've come to the
conclusion, man, that I'm
part of the problem."

NAME: Romeo

AGE: 5

HOBBY: Restoring old VW buses

"Sometimes I think I'm an embarrassment to my entire species."

NAME: Misha

AGE: 5

HOBBY: Apologizing to non-dogs

"She'll be comin' round the mountain when she comes. All together now!"

NAME: Tina
AGE: 3
HOBBY: Making homemade scrunchies

"C'mon out, Checkers. We promise--all we're going to do is lick each other."

NAMES: Shiloh and Lily Claire
AGES: 9, 3
HOBBY: Greco-Roman wrestling

"This is where I come at night to pick up schnauzers."

NAME: Budweiser

AGE: 6

HOBBY: Earning Boy Scout badges

"There's *nothin'* I won't put my nose in."

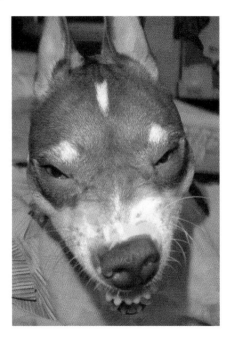

NAME: **Foxi**

AGE: **3**

HOBBY: **Barking at the door even when I don't need to go out**

"Mr. and Mrs. Tuthill don't live here anymore."

NAME: Woody

AGE: 13

HOBBY: Looking at photos of naked dolls

"They call me Paulie 'No Nuts.'"

NAME: Marley

AGE: 3

HOBBY: Surf fishing

"You can either open the door, or I can do it somewhere where you won't find it for a week. Your choice."

NAME: Sandy
AGE: 7 months
HOBBY: Dead languages

"I'm self-watering."

NAME: Munchkin

AGE: 3

HOBBY: Wine cork art

"As soon as I've made
fifty thousand more, the
universe is mine. Mine,
I tell you!"

NAME: Dr. Gorby

AGE: 7

HOBBY: Geopolitics

"I only make love with the lights on."

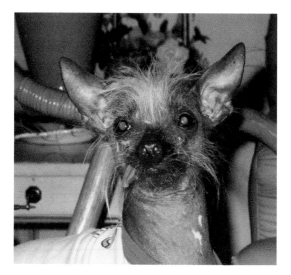

NAME: Zippy

AGE: 7

HOBBY: Gardening in the nude

"After a big bean dinner, my wife prefers I nap on the deck."

NAME: Schatten

AGE: 2

HOBBY: Bushwhacking

"Tonight, I want to be the warden."

NAME: Bandel

AGE: 9

HOBBY: Large format origami

"Let's talk later--*Desperate Housewives* is starting."

NAME: Shadow

AGE: 7

HOBBY: Repairing old housecoats

"I'm offering you the lead
in my next films, baby:
Lay Her Like a Tramp and
On Golden Retriever."

NAME: Johnny Javelin
AGE: 11
HOBBY: Residential real
estate

"Let me get this straight:
You want to *what* me like a
rabbit?"

NAME: Hannah
AGE: 12
HOBBY: Imaginary astronomy

"The key to chasing cars is not getting too close to the bumpers."

NAME: Kakunoshin

AGE: 3

HOBBY: Coupon club

"Put the steak down, step away from the grill, and you won't get hurt."

NAMES: High Five and Maynard
AGES: 11, 7
HOBBY: Sorting scraps

"Ten bucks is fine, but I'm gonna need a bath first."

NAME: The Beaz

AGE: 15

HOBBY: Twitching even when awake

"Under here, in my special
place, is where I can
really enjoy my gas."

NAME: Sinbad

AGE: 6 months

HOBBY: Playing the dulcimer

"When you drink like I do,
every day is Mardi Gras."

NAME: Blanche
AGE: 10
HOBBY: Dixieland clarinet

"A judicious application of urine has rendered these flowers yellow."

NAME: Pansy Pooh

AGE: 7

HOBBY: Dioramas of 19th century dogs chasing buggies

"My New Year's resolution--
stop blacking out."

NAME: Sugar

AGE: 3

HOBBY: Mojito support group

"Please don't tell the
other guard dogs."

NAME: Paddy Wack
AGE: 6
HOBBY: Monitoring The
Weather Channel

"Whoa! Room's spinnin' good now!"

NAME: Sam

AGE: 5

HOBBY: Skim boarding

"See you in hell."

NAME: Bullseye
AGE: 7
HOBBY: Scratch golf

"I'll let you know when it's okay to pet me."

NAME: Sadie

AGE: 5

HOBBY: Chewing priceless family photos

"Let's see, if I'm not mistaken, that would be the Gunderson's rottweiler's heinie?"

NAME: Buddy

AGE: 4 months

HOBBY: *Winky Dink and You* memorabilia

"In January, I'll be raising my fee to $165 an hour."

NAME: Milo Klaidman, Ph.D.

AGE: 2

HOBBY: Restoring leather love seats

"Do you have any idea what
time it is, young lady?
You're grounded."

NAME: Sammi
AGE: 13
HOBBY: Weed whacking

"It's gonna take a pretty big pooper-scooper to clean up this town."

NAME: Randy

AGE: 3

HOBBY: Playing the button accordian

"That's because the cowhands just can't git enough of Thunder Mae's special bean-and-horse-meat chili."

NAME: Thunder Mae
AGE: 4
HOBBY: Wagon wheel chandelier repair

"I made it myself."

NAME: Harvey

AGE: 4

HOBBY: Learning to speak "cat"

"Beat it. I don't talk to
reporters from The Stuffed
Animal Channel."

NAME: Calvin

AGE: 8

HOBBY: Designing own line of
muzzles

"Twenty bucks, big boy.
Twenty-five if we let the
pumpkins watch."

NAME: Maritza
AGE: 5
HOBBY: Leg waxing

"On our next date, I'll show you the other half of it."

NAME: Jake

AGE: 1

HOBBY: Bumper pool

"Oakley, you rock my world.
Now I know why they call
you *Great* Danes."

NAMES: Tiny and Oakley
AGES: 3, 7
HOBBY: Designing canine wax
museum

"After seeing patients for 11 months, these weeks in August on the Cape are a godsend."

NAME: Hunter

AGE: 10

HOBBY: Researching dogs of antiquity

"How does the scene go again, Marty? The nurse enters, takes my pulse, and *then* I take off the pants?"

NAME: Lance

AGE: 1

HOBBY: Air hockey

"You and me, Harry, one-on-one, right here, right now."

NAME: Richie

AGE: 5

HOBBY: Dribbling

"Say you're sorry for
sleeping on my blanky."

NAME: Bodie

AGE: 7

HOBBY: Learning the oboe

"Smoke, blow, 'shrooms. I can take you anywhere you wanna go, baby."

NAME: Wheezer
AGE: 8
HOBBY: Motown historian

"I've consulted with Zortan. You must be sacrificed."

NAME: Sanford

AGE: 2

HOBBY: Listening to the music of Uranus

"I'm the gift that keeps on giving--check under the kitchen table."

NAME: Dillon

AGE: 1

HOBBY: Belly dancing

"I love costume orgies."

NAME: Cooler

AGE: 7

HOBBY: Mange research

"It was harmless, honey---a couple of drinks and a lap dance."

NAME: Wheatie

AGE: 2

HOBBY: Watching Spectravision

"Why would anyone wipe
with this stuff when they
can eat it?"

NAME: Lucy
AGE: 10 months
HOBBY: Water ballet

"I've got the bong--who brought the weed?"

NAME: Lubee

AGE: 6 months

HOBBY: Trading Grateful Dead bootlegs

"Nice tiles. Now see if you
can find my vomit."

NAME: Kereina
AGE: 1
HOBBY: Claymation

"She love me long time."

NAME: Gizmo

AGE: 3

HOBBY: Watching classic romance movies on laser disc

"They say the seventh
marriage is a charm."

NAME: Sasha

AGE: 2

HOBBY: Key parties in the
Hamptons

"Do you miss nursing as
much as I do?"

NAMES: Ruby and Dora
AGES: 8 weeks
HOBBY: Jug band music

"I couldn't hold it. C'est
la vie."

NAME: Petey
AGE: 6 months
HOBBY: Airline courier

"This community started going downhill as soon as they allowed cats in."

NAME: Lara Bear

AGE: 3

HOBBY: President of the Welcome Wagon

"Your toilet should flush
fine now, Mrs. Orlowsky."

NAMES: Bucky and Charles
AGES: 6, 11
HOBBY: Spelunking

"Wait a second--is that your vomit, or mine?"

NAMES: Rudy and Roxy
AGES: 6 months
HOBBY: Watching reruns of *Full House*

"Do these jeans make my butt look big?"

NAME: Hector

AGE: 4

HOBBY: Suicide hotline volunteer

"The younger generation
doesn't care about money,
or what it can buy."

NAME: Louie

AGE: 13

HOBBY: Victorian pornography

"If you're wondering, it tastes like chicken."

NAME: Trixie

AGE: 9 weeks

HOBBY: Searching for distant galaxies

"Yo yo homey, word up."

NAME: Rufhausen

AGE: 14 months

HOBBY: Pruning

"I'll tell you what I want,
Santa. I want to hump your
leg."

NAME: Chloe Anne
AGE: 8 weeks
HOBBY: Balinese chanting

"If only I could speak hen,
I'd tell her how much I
love hen."

NAME: Tassja

AGE: 7

HOBBY: Threshing

"I know I look fresh as a daisy, but smell my tongue."

NAME: Patty

AGE: 3

HOBBY: Scrap metal sculpture

"Sometimes I wonder if all
the therapy was worth it."

NAME: Boss

AGE: 2

HOBBY: Making pencil caddies
out of soup cans

"That fifth dirty martini
is a bitch."

NAME: Jessie Lee
AGE: 2
HOBBY: Designating drivers

"Stop licking the cards, Champ."

NAMES: **Maxie and Champ**
AGES: **8, 5**
HOBBY: **Hand-polishing wood floors**

"My teeth aren't just clean.
They're Colgate clean."

NAME: Abbi
AGE: 6 months
HOBBY: Mountain biking

"School sucks. My parents blow. And this suburb bites the big one."

NAME: Bruce

AGE: 7

HOBBY: Tractor-mower racing

"When you hear the tinkle,
I'm tinkling."

NAME: LuLu

AGE: 2

HOBBY: Gourmet macrobiotic
cooking

"Humma, humma--get a load
of those coconuts!"

NAME: Van
AGE: 1
HOBBY: Watching classic
boxing movies

"I'm a bipolar cowboy."

NAME: Cinder

AGE: 2

HOBBY: Saloon tours

"I love the smell of her cheap perfume."

NAME: Al
AGE: 1
HOBBY: Window-shopping at the Goodwill

"Jump in--the urine's fine."

NAME: Travis

AGE: 8

HOBBY: Claw-hammer banjo plucking

"I call this Operation Get Me the Hell Out of This Costume."

NAME: Hershey

AGE: 2

HOBBY: Fetching Kevlar

"I wish candied yams
weren't so binding."

NAMES: Spencer and Molly
AGES: 13, 7
HOBBY: Annual pilgrimages to
Plimouth Plantation

"You're my cousin, and this
is wrong, but you smell
like heaven."

NAMES: David and Rosie
AGES: 7, 3
HOBBY: Weekends away

"They make me wear the mask so I don't scare the children."

NAME: Brewster Earl

AGE: 5

HOBBY: Licking infants

"I lost my bottom half to an enormous bluefish."

NAME: Chit-chat
AGE: 1
HOBBY: Baiting telemarketers

"I left a Yankee Doodle
dandy in your bedroom."

NAME: Matilda
AGE: 9
HOBBY: Quilting

"You've tried the rest. Now try the best."

NAME: Kyle
AGE: 11
HOBBY: Giving facials

"Hey! You in the rhinestone collar! Have you ever done zero to sixty with a bulldog?"

NAME: Forrest

AGE: 3

HOBBY: Learning to whistle

"Mirror, mirror, on the
wall, who's the most
neutered of them all?"

NAME: Dozier
AGE: 1
HOBBY: Macaroni art

"You're gonna love this one:
three Shih Tzus walk into
a bar--tell me if ya heard
this one already."

NAME: Ditto

AGE: 7

HODDY: Picking fights with
Seeing Eye dogs

"Heeeere's Johnny!"

NAME: Johnny Awesome

AGE: 4

HOBBY: Reading magazines
upside down

"That smell? That would be me. Silent but deadly."

NAME: Jake
AGE: 8 weeks
HOBBY: Player piano restoration

"So much for the Circle of Life."

NAME: Dandee

AGE: 7

HOBBY: Watching The Plumbers Channel

"I'd like to roast *your* chestnuts on an open fire."

NAME: Snowball
AGE: 10
HOBBY: Discus

"I never wiped before."

NAME: Penny

AGE: 3

HOBBY: Slow-pitch softball

"I am *so* baked."

NAME: Puddin

AGE: 1

HOBBY: Watching *F Troop* reruns

"Like I said, one hit is all you need."

NAME: Murray

AGE: 1

HOBBY: Chasing skunks

"I had a six-year affair with my pastor."

NAME: Itsy Marie

AGE: 16

HOBBY: Baking bone-shaped cakes

"I was prima ballerina
until I lost the feeling
in my back legs."

NAME: Daisy
AGE: 8 months
HOBBY: Jowl massage

"I only go in the game
when coach wants to use
the old 'pass gas' play."

NAME: Chance

AGE: 5

HOBBY: Surfing the 'net for
other people with my name

"Get your own damn beer,
ya fat lump."

NAME: Roberta

AGE: 10

HOBBY: Collecting Polaroid
Land cameras

"God, I love that Bill O'Reilly."

NAME: Lester

AGE: 4

HOBBY: Vacationing in Red States

"I don't fetch during
'Stairway to Heaven.'"

NAME: Raydar
AGE: 5
HOBBY: Glassblowing

"Sorry to interrupt your dinner, sir, but I'm with the EPA and we've been tracking a foul odor."

NAME: Fearless Fred XII

AGE: 2

HOBBY: Traditional Vietnamese cooking

"We're into swapping. How about you guys?"

NAMES: Ola and Rodney
AGES: 1, 2
HOBBY: Hot-tubbing

"How. I'm Chief Ticks in My Ear."

NAME: Chief Ticks in My Ear

AGE: 14

HOBBY: Building sweat kennels

"No one understands me.
That's why I kill."

NAME: Gunter

AGE: 4

HOBBY: Sharpening cutlery

"'Fetch this!' 'Fetch that!'
What do I look like, a
freakin' yellow Lab?"

NAME: Terence

AGE: 7

HOBBY: Poetry slams

"Who you callin' Granny?"

NAME: Fiona

AGE: 2

HOBBY: Shoplifting at yard sales

"If I were a female, I'm sure I would find this more enjoyable."

NAME: Kirk

AGE: 6

HOBBY: TiVo-ing *Animal Rescue*

"Eight years on the force--
and the smell of a crime
scene still excites me."

NAME: Graf

AGE: 10

HOBBY: Fixing broken radios

"Bring me Dopey."

NAME: Gypsy

AGE: 10

HOBBY: Collecting Bruno Bettelheim first editions

"There's no tackling in the Chihuahua League--just nipping, yapping, and shivering."

NAME: Baslow

AGE: 1

HOBBY: Snowmobile racing

"Dead dog walkin'."

NAME: Moby

AGE: 2

HOBBY: Reading *Outdoor Life* magazine

"I'll do anything for a turkey wing."

NAME: Ellie

AGE: 6

HOBBY: Copyediting

"This is bad bone, and I'm trippin'."

NAME: Copper
AGE: 4 months
HOBBY: Crashing chat rooms

"You have to admit it looks real."

NAME: Stephen
AGE: 12
HOBBY: Collecting tin soldiers

"What's my cure for depression?
Two words: Jim Beam."

NAME: Bert

AGE: 10

HOBBY: Listening only to
Philip Glass music

"I don't live in Deadwood.
I *am* dead wood."

NAME: Chewy
AGE: 7
HOBBY: Ambling

"I don't want the government telling me who, what, when, or where to lick."

NAME: Bongo

AGE: 10

HOBBY: Planning parade routes

"Thank god you're here,
man. I've been smoking
seeds."

NAME: Oreo

AGE: 4

HOBBY: Tweezing chin hairs

"Ever since I got fixed,
you've been so distant."

NAMES: Cassie and Dwight
AGES: 10, 4
HOBBY: Japanese rock
gardening

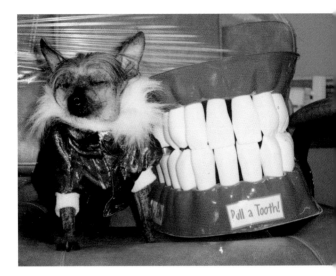

"Here's how it works: Take
off your clothes, put on
the teeth, and I'll get
the ointment."

NAME: Ah-Tay
AGE: 2
HOBBY: Raising koi

"Get a friggin' tree next year, you cheap bastards!"

NAME: Spunky

AGE: 5

HOBBY: Waiting for Kwanzaa

"How do you know it's mine?
Did you smell it?"

NAME: Heidi
AGE: 4 months
HOBBY: Spitball competitions

"This is what I wear when I hump dogs I don't know."

NAME: Larry

AGE: 3

HOBBY: Antique watch collecting

"There are still a lot of
dogs who like a whippet
with big hair."

NAME: Lucille
AGE: 3
HOBBY: Saving up for a
ThighMaster

"I just felt my ball drop."

NAMES: Noel and Reggie
AGES: 5, 4
HOBBY: Playing hide-and-seek
with garden gnomes

"What does it look like
I've been eating?"

NAME: Angel
AGE: 8 months
HOBBY: Curling

"The name of my one-dog play? *Spayed by an Angel.*"

NAME: Donald

AGE: 3

HOBBY: Ionesco memorabilia

"Ah, summer. There's nothing like the smell of rotting garbage, old piss, and dogs in heat."

NAME: Scout

AGE: 4

HOBBY: Shuffling cards

"I'm having a thing with
the bearded lady."

NAME: Mulligan

AGE: 1

HOBBY: Small-town values

"Nothing against rodents,
but would you mind if I
turned off the lights?"

NAME: Bismarck
AGE: 1
HOBBY: Tracing Edward Hopper
prints

"Okay--this one smells clean."

NAME: Tucker

AGE: 12

HOBBY: Working on my second serve

"Heh-heh. We don't know about Rudolph's nose, but his butt sure is red."

NAMES: (l. to r.) La Quinta, Demi, Harvest, and Candi
AGES: 7, 2, 10, 11
HOBBY: Meat-smoking club

"Guns don't kill pheasants.
Pheasants kill pheasants."

NAME: Wally

AGE: 4

HOBBY: Model airplanes

"To be honest, Barbara,
you're not a thong person."

NAME: Cody

AGE: 8

HOBBY: Abdominal crunches

"Ahh, now that's what a flower *should* smell like!"

NAME: Trinket

AGE: 3

HOBBY: Long, hot, soapy baths

"The champagne is dry, but
my pants are wet."

NAME: Scooby
AGE: 8
HOBBY: Illustrating books for
puppies

"Being a crash-test doggie isn't for everyone, but I have to make a buck somehow."

NAME: Samson

AGE: 2

HOBBY: Reading canine martial arts magazines

"This bedspread smells
like your ex."

NAME: Tofu

AGE: 7

HOBBY: Trying to legally
change name

"Ahh, Fifi."

NAME: Morgan

AGE: 7

HOBBY: Applying to student exchange programs

"Why didn't you just tell
me I spit when I talk?"

NAMES: Kiki and Nick
AGES: 2, 8 months
HOBBY: Restoring cobblestone
paths

"I'm suing *Extreme Makeover*."

NAME: Honey

AGE: 1

HOBBY: Moving around as little as possible

"This diaper can't hold
much more."

NAME: Ginger

AGE: 2 weeks

HOBBY: Resisting Ferberization

"Don't piss me off."

NAME: Molly

AGE: 3

HOBBY: Watching Steven Seagal movies

"That big, fat sonofabitch
fired me!"

NAME: Kirby

AGE: 10 months

HOBBY: Luge

"Is this enough of an answer for you?"

NAME: Helen

AGE: 13

HOBBY: Watching *Jeopardy* in syndication

"Just keep walking,
gringo."

NAME: José
AGE: 5
HOBBY: 12-string guitar

"Let's just say I've made some bad choices. Now how 'bout that drink?"

NAME: Rylee

AGE: 9

HOBBY: Cooking with Sterno

"In Paris without pants. . . .
Is there anything better?"

NAME: Jennifer

AGE: 3

HOBBY: Embroidering passport
cases

"I know, I know. The nose takes it a step too far."

NAME: Cachou

AGE: 10

HOBBY: Impersonating bigger dogs

"Welcome to my temple of sensual delights."

NAME: Charlie Jessen
AGE: 1
HOBBY: Creating incense for toy breeds

"Lawrence always said he was going to be hit by a truck."

NAME: Bella

AGE: 5 months

HOBBY: Hospital volunteer work

"Please. I have a shy
bladder."

NAME: Milly

AGE: 2

HOBBY: Bird-watching

"Eddie, I'd have to say
that Mexican food doesn't
agree with you."

NAME: Sidney

AGE: 3

HOBBY: Hand-sewing moccasins

"Kiss me like there's no tomorrow."

NAME: Lily

AGE: 2

HOBBY: Enjoying a crackling fire and hot cocoa

NOTE: We would like to thank all the dog owners whose photographs, creativity, and, in some cases, shameless treatment of their pets made this book possible. We would also like to thank all the dogs for allowing us to use their images, even though many of them have nothing to gain from the publicity. By the way, none of the photographs in this book have been retouched or altered in any way, although a couple of them, we have reason to believe, are upside-down.

244

About the Authors

R. D. ROSEN is an Edgar Award-winning mystery novelist and a humorist whose work has appeared in book form (*Not Available In Any Store*), on television (PBS, HBO, CBS), and--with partner Harry Prichett--on National Public Radio's "All Things Considered."

HARRY PRICHETT has written and performed for the improv comedy groups Chicago City Limits and Radio Active Theater, is the creator of the off-off-Broadway one-man show *Work=Pain= Success,* and has appeared on television and in film.

ROB BATTLES writes about music and pain abatement, has written and produced for public radio stations and NPR, and has relied on humor to avoid beatings since the third grade. He currently works in commercial television promotion.

Together, with Jim Edgar, they wrote the #1 *New York Times* bestseller *Bad Cat.*

Bad Dog Warning Signs

If your dog is going bad, we want to know about it. Send us a photo of your dog if:

* Any prescription medicine is missing from your cabinet

* Your Scotch tastes watered down

* You can't find your stiletto heels

* She calls out another owner's name in her sleep

* There are tooth marks on the prosciutto

* His breath smells of cigarettes

* Your son can't find his Dracula costume

* Your best thong is missing

* Your credit card statement includes an $89 charge for wholesale meat products

* She often leaves the house without saying where she's going

* You find cat porn behind the dog bed

* He's wearing mascara

* She comes home with an expensive new leash

* He's humping the vacuum cleaner